SUCHNESS

Richard von Sturmer is a New Zealand writer who has had published two books, *We Xerox Your Zebras* (Modern House, 1988) and *A Network of Dissolving Threads* (Auckland University Press, 1991). As well as being a lyricist for several New Zealand bands, including Blam Blam Blam, he and his wife, Amala Wrightson, toured the country in the 1980s as the performing duo, The Humanimals. From 1993 to 2003 he lived and worked at the Rochester Zen Center, a Buddhist community in upstate New York. During that time his work appeared regularly in literary journals and anthologies. He has now returned to live in New Zealand.

Also by Richard von Sturmer

We Xerox Your Zebras
A Network of Dissolving Threads

Suchness

Zen Poetry and Prose

Richard von Sturmer

HEADWORX
WELLINGTON

For Amala

First published 2005
HeadworX Publishers
97/43 Mulgrave Street
Thorndon, Wellington
Aotearoa / New Zealand

http://headworx.eyesis.co.nz

ISBN 0-476-01030-6

Printed by Astra Print, Wellington

Cover photograph by Richard von Sturmer

Cover design and book design by Derek Ward

Photographs by Richard von Sturmer

Published with the assistance of a grant from

creative nz

Arts Council of New Zealand Toi Aotearoa

CONTENTS

INTRODUCTION

This collection is drawn from my writings over the past ten years, a period in which I was based in upstate New York, living and working at the Rochester Zen Center, a Buddhist community.

The *Zen Poetry* section has a direct connection to Zen practice, with *Mumonkan Verses* and *Blue Cliff Verses* arising from my formal work on koans. Zen Buddhism has a long history of producing literary works related to koans, and I trust that these verses stand on their own. However, for readers unfamiliar with Buddhist terminology, a glossary is provided.

Haiku Notebooks reflect the four distinct seasons experienced in Rochester, with the emphasis on winter, which lasts at least five months. As well as *Winter at Chapin Mill*, the coldest season also makes its presence felt in the tanka sequence *Winter Shadows*.

The tanka sequence *Barrier Crossings*, written on Great Barrier Island, marks my return to New Zealand in 2003, while *Reflections* was composed at a friend's house near Pakiri Beach, on the East Coast between Auckland and Whangarei.

The two closing essays, *Time and Light* and *The Bodhisattvic Garden*, come from my residency at the Rochester Zen Center.

I would like to express my gratitude to Sensei Amala Wrightson, Roshi Bodhin Kjolhede, Roshi Philip Kapleau, David Goldfarb, Ian Harnett, John Geraets, Jack Ross, and Derek Ward for their support.

Pieces in this collection have appeared in the following publications:
Zen Bow, *Frogpond*, *brief*, *Sport*, *Landfall*, *JAAM*, and *The New Zealand Listener*; and on the Internet at: www.mudlark.com, www.muse-apprentice-guild.com, www.linnaenstreet.com/

ZEN POEMS

DHARMA VERSES

Justice
just is.

The just is
of a sparrow.
The just is
of a lamppost.

Everything
obeys the Law.

*

The world is vast
like the dark hallway
of my grandmother's house.
The house vanished
many years ago
and still the world is vast.

*

Self-esteem:
there is no self
to esteem.
The fork is bent.
The knife is straight.

The Three Disabilities

all beings are deaf:
the incoming tide
carries seaweed
to the back of the cave

*

all beings are dumb:
the sharp nib
of the fountain pen
just scratches the paper

*

all beings are blind:
the weight of the snow
removes the last leaves
from the gingko

In This Dream World

In this dream world
being crushed
by the doors of hell
not knowing
if I'm coming in
or going out.

*

In this dream world
one interlude
follows the next
with such sweetness
that I forget
if something
was meant to happen.

*

In this dream world
a pheasant cries
from deep in the bush.

Each day the same voice.
Each day a different place.

Zazen

desolate zazen:
my shadow on the wall
continues to sit

*

exhausted zazen:
a moth flits
from mat to mat

*

twilight zazen:
we're all
bones and shadows

Sesshin

Manjusri dances
between the candles.
His black sword
reflects no light
and yet
everything is ablaze.

Yaza

Late at night
below the back deck
the white dots of daisies
silently become
a scattering of stars.

Stretching out my legs
I'm at the edge of the universe.

The Life of the Buddha

Shakyamuni's Birth

'Above the heavens, below the heavens
I am the only one.'

The words were fresh, linen
sheets billowed in the wind.
A washing basket lay nearby
like a small ship beached on dry land.
And as the newborn moved forward
confidently, step by step
the clouds overhead compressed
and sent down
the finest shower of rain.

Shakyamuni's Awakening

The morning star
was already there
through his great exertion
through each bead
of perspiration
through the buzzing of cicadas
and the swirling of dust.

The morning star was there
just waiting to be seen.

Shakyamuni Proclaims the Dharma

They didn't shift their weight
from side to side
or, reaching back,
run their beaks through their feathers.
This ancient assembly
with wrinkled necks and bald heads
squatted motionless on the rock
and simply listened
to each unfolding sentence
uttered by the Buddha
on Vulture Peak.

Shakyamuni's Parinirvana

When he lay down and died
it was rather disturbing
how the demons shed tears
along with the gods in heaven
and the animals on the earth.

But his death was just
another opening.
And all of us, at that moment,
became a little more human
with our horns and halos
scattered in the long grass.

The Six Realms

Hell Realm

unrelenting heat:
with this fever
each falling petal
burns the flesh

*

Hungry Ghost Realm

screech of a hawk,
the wind swirls
clouds of snow
across the frozen pond

*

Animal Realm

increasing cold:
throughout the afternoon
a wasp keeps walking
around the rim of a cup

Asura Realm

dark summer rain,
inside the zendo
the smell of incense
the sound of thunder

*

Human Realm

on the ceiling
of a rented room
blue light flickers
from a black and white T.V.

*

Deva Realm

the horse chestnut
flings up
pagodas of blossoms
fifty feet into the sky

black swan:
its eyes as red
as its beak

even on a still morning
my karmic forces
keep circulating

*

striking the big bell
at the end of the year:
everything goes . . .
everything comes back

*

cu-ru-cu cu-cu
the mourning dove calls
out of the darkness
I can think of no response—
all my words have gone away

MUMONKAN VERSES

The Buddha Holds up a Flower

From the outside, Shakyamuni
appears to raise up Kashyapa
while the monks in their silence
are like silt.

But in the depths
each contains a grain of pollen
each bears the light of many stars.

Daitsu Chisho

When I enter the zendo
late at night
a solitary figure
sits facing the wall.

We can all be grateful
in the hours before dawn
that Daitsu Chisho
is doing zazen.

Nansen Cuts the Cat in Two

Nansen:
Slicing the cat with a single stroke
and sprinkling its blood
on the monastery grounds:
this is the way you instruct your monks,
their hearts in their mouths
their hands palm to palm.

Joshu:
Placing a sandal on your head
and letting that sandal extend
until it covers the sky:
this is the way you take your leave
your conduct in harmony
with the moon and the clouds.

The Sound of the Bell and the Seven-Piece Robe

It's all right to ask why
so long as that why
is as vast as the universe
with each thing
its own answer:

table and book
bell and robe.

Tozan and "Three Pounds of Flax"

Three Pounds of Flax!
Three Pounds of Flax!
The flax is black and tastes bitter.
It gets under your fingernails
and works its way behind your eyes.

Three Pounds of Flax!
Three Pounds of Flax!
Water becomes fire.
Fire becomes iron.

A Man of Great Strength

As I look at him
he looks back at me.
I don't know who he is
but he knows who I am.

This man of great strength
balanced on a leaf
swaying gently in the breeze.

Two Monks Roll Up the Bamboo Blinds

'One has it,
the other does not.'
Shadows fall
both East and West.

At midnight
the crack
that splits the windowpane
sparkles like a river
in the light of the moon.

Ryutan Blows Out a Candle

Mid-summer's
candle flame
fire-hydrant
yellow.

At the cawing of a crow
the centuries collapse
like a folding screen.

Joshu Sees Through the Old Woman

Kannon wears a hearing-aid.
Fugen walks with a limp.
Seems like we're all
on the road to Mt. Gotai.

Tottering
shuffling
stumbling forward –
becoming
more transparent
at each step.

Not Mind, Not Buddha

I'm just a snake with horns
scraping them against the walls
of a long, dark tunnel.

Someday I'll reach daylight
and in the sky there'll be
a dragon-headed cloud.

Kicking over the Water Bottle

My last day at primary school:
kicking an empty ink bottle
into the long grass.

The whistle of a train
shimmers in the background.

Many years later,
Isan's water bottle appears
and I hold it up to the light.

Tosotsu's Three Barriers

Making your way across
an uncultivated field
numerous small crickets
jump out of your path.

Glistening with dew
the blackness of their bodies
belongs to the night.

And in that night
when your eyes no longer see
and your ears perceive no sound
the crickets will continue to chirp
beneath a sky filled with stars.

BLUE CLIFF VERSES

Baso is Unwell

Sun-faced Buddha:
persimmon
pineapple
papaya.

Moon-faced Buddha:
syringe
stethoscope
scalpel.

While on the bedside table
a glass of water holds
the early-morning light.

Joshu's Four Gates

Through the east gate
you'll find a desert.
Through the west gate
there's a field of wheat.
Through the north gate
rise jagged mountains.
Through the south gate
lies the deep blue sea.

Who knows for sure
where Joshu has gone.
In the abandoned courtyard
hens and chickens scratch the earth.

Haryo's Snow in a Silver Bowl

My left hand
lies beside me on the pillow.

Snowflakes drift
through the open window.

In this dream of winter
embers and cinders
intermingle.

A discarded glove
gathers dust
at the bottom of the stairs.

The National Teacher's Seamless Monument

Ah, those old masters,
they can extract your heart
with a single phrase.

And everything appears
veiled—
cars, houses, streets,
all covered by a fine mist.

And your own heart beating
faintly
in the wing-beats of a sparrow.

Seppo's Turtle-Nosed Snake

While seated in zazen
small wings grow
from the tips of your elbows
lifting you high into the air,
setting you down on South Mountain
before the serpent.

A string of saliva
hangs from its jaws.
You wrap it around your finger
as if it were candy floss.

Daizui's "It Goes Along with Everything Else"

It's like a blind man and his dog,
the dog leads,
and the blind man follows.

It could also be said
that people who descend
into volcanoes
are not necessarily
vulcanologists.

One blast from the furnace
strips away
skin from flesh
and flesh from bone.

Joshu's Big Radishes

Joshu holds up his radishes
for everyone to see.
But look at the earth –
How it encrusts the white skin!
How it clings to the wispy roots!

This gritty, crumbling,
uncompromising earth.

I thought that I entered Zen
to attain the pure sky,
but each day I find myself
buried deeper underground.

Manjusri's Threes and Threes

Mujaku:
It's like trying to use
a dirty eraser:
the more you rub out
the more you smudge the page.

Manjusri:
It's like looking through
a diamond window:
each facet reveals
ten thousand details.

Joshu and the Great Death

Night will turn into day.
The tin cans will gleam
in their recycling bins
and the crows
torn away from the darkness
will begin to caw.

If death were then
to make an appearance
he would be somewhat insignificant:
a piece of broken tile
a frayed doormat
the handle of a broom.

Sansho's Golden Carp Out of the Net

At the mud-splattered window
for less than a second
the face of a fish.

Under the swaying trees
a shifting pattern
of shadows and light.

All you can tell me
is that the midday heat
has left you exhausted.

In the distance
someone plays a violin.

Joshu's Stone Bridge

In the middle of a long journey
I stand on Joshu's stone bridge
with sore legs and an aching back.

The points of light overhead
are almost too faint to be called stars.
And you would have difficulty
describing the water below.
Is it sluggish or simply meandering?
Is it tar-black, or does it retain
a trace of purple?

Near the opposite bank
where the reeds are brushed together
a pair of ducks glides downstream.

Dogo's "I Won't Say"

I won't say
if the sperm fertilizes the egg
although the moon is above
and the earth is below.

I won't say
where the crow sleeps at night
although the wind is cold
and the snow is wet.

I won't say tenderness.
I won't say forgetfulness.
I won't say.

Ummon's Staff Turns into a Dragon

Ummon's staff is no less than
a magic wand.

With a single tap a toaster
turns into a toaster
and a teacup
becomes a teacup.

Through the power of the staff
you can see in broad daylight
and receive the sounds
of insects
and small birds.

Ummon's One Treasure

The Eiffel Tower
bounces on a trampoline.
The Sphinx comes inside
for her bowl of milk.

Ummon says,
'Take the temple gate and place it on the lamp.'

The earth trembles, the sky vibrates . . .

And on the washing-line
it's still Saturday
with the clothes hanging
good-naturedly
from their wooden pegs.

Kingyu's Rice Pail

Leaves fall
—the bell is rung—
more leaves fall.

Some are ashamed
when they eat the rice.
Others just eat the rice.
Others eat the bowl as well.

Leaves fall
—the bell is rung—
more leaves fall.

Sixteen Bodhisattvas Enter the Bath

Right down
"full fathom five"
a deep joy resides
with crustaceans
and anemones
and rocks collected
from early childhood.

Water bodhisattvas.
Aquasattvas.

On the bath-mat
a wet footprint
slowly evaporates.

Ummon's "Everyone Has His Own Light"

The shortest day:
dark in the morning
dark in the afternoon.

Outside some skeletons
are playing in the snow.
Their bones must be cold,
so very cold—and yet
they're eager for us to join their game.

'Come out of the shadows!
Come down to the gate!
Everyone is welcome here.
Everyone has his own light.'

The Hands and Eyes of Kannon

The eye smells the incense.
The eye tastes the persimmon.
The eye hears the voices of children in a courtyard
and the barking of a dog.

Overhead geese are flying
in the late autumn sky.
The hand touches their soft feathers,
feels the beating of their hearts.

And when a film of ice covers the bare branches
the one who has been attending
adjusts the weight of her pack
and descends into the valley.

Joshu's Three Turning Words

'A clay Buddha cannot pass through water.'
Clouds of mud
and inside the clouds
atoms of mud.

'A wooden Buddha cannot pass through fire.'
The hiss of resin
a red crevasse –
everything splits apart.

'A metal Buddha cannot pass through a furnace.'
Dented moonlight
melting down
to the last sliver.

Haryo and a Blown Hair Against a Sword

In this dream world
of trucks and pigeons
and income tax,
reality becomes
the beeping of a horn
the fluttering of wings
the adding up of figures.

In this dream world
of endless desires
we drift through the stillness
of a vast ocean
among swords and sponges
starfish and feathers.

ZEN BUDDHIST GLOSSARY

Asura. Fighting god or titan. The Asura realm, usually below that of heaven, is one of the Six Realms of unenlightened existence.

Bodhisattva. An enlightened being who guides others to enlightenment. A bodhisattva renounces complete entry into Nirvana until all beings are liberated.

Buddha. The Enlightened One, 'one who is awake'. Buddha usually refers to the historical Buddha, Shakyamuni.

Daitsu Chisho. A non-historical Buddha who appears in the *Lotus Sutra*. Daitsu Chisho did not achieve enlightenment even though he sat in zazen for countless eons.

Deva. A heavenly being. The Deva realm is one of the Six Realms of unenlightened existence.

Dharma. The Law or the Ultimate Truth. Dharma is also the teaching of the Buddha. With a lower-case "d", dharma simply means "phenomenon" or "thing".

Fugen. The Japanese name for Samantabhadra, the Bodhisattva of enlightened action. Literally, 'he who is all-pervading good'.

Joshu. The Japanese name for the great Chinese master, Zhaozhou (778-879). Zhaozhou only began teaching at the age of eighty.

Kannon. The Japanese name for Avalokiteshvara, the Bodhisattva of great compassion. Literally, 'one who hears the sounds of the world'. Guanyin is her Chinese name.

Kashyapa. The shortened form of Mahakashyapa, one of the main disciples of the Buddha. Kashyapa took over the leadership of the monastic community after the Buddha's death.

Koan. Literally a 'public case'. A testing story or question that forces the Zen student to leap beyond the rational mind and see into the true nature of reality.

Manjusri. The Bodhisattva of wisdom. Manjusri is often depicted wielding a delusion-cutting sword.

Mt. Gotai. The Japanese name for Wutai Shan, one of the five sacred mountains of China. Wutai Shan is believed to be the abode of Manjusri.

Mujaku. The Japanese name for Wu Cho, a Zen student who travelled widely before becoming a teacher.

Mumonkan. *The Gateless Barrier*. One of the two most important collections of koans (the other being the *Hekiganroku* or *Blue Cliff Record*).

Parinirvana. Literally, 'complete extinction'. The term is frequently used to describe the passing away of the Buddha.

Sesshin. An intense retreat of Zen meditation, traditionally lasting seven days.

Shakyamuni. Literally, 'Sage of the Shakya Clan'. The name of the historical Buddha.

Six Realms. The realms of hell, hungry ghosts, animals, asuras, human beings, and devas. The Six Realms form the wheel of birth-and-death on which the unenlightened keep revolving.

Ummon. The Japanese name for the Chinese master, Yunmen (864-949). Yunmen's pithy sayings are esteemed by the Zen school.

Vulture Peak. In Sanskrit, Mount Grdhrakuta. The mountain on which the Buddha expounded many of his teachings.

Yaza. Informal, late night sitting during a meditation retreat.

Zazen. The practice of Zen meditation.

Zen. Focused meditation or absorption (*dhyana* in Sanskrit, and *chan* in Chinese). A school of Mahayana Buddhism.

Zendo. A room or hall where zazen is practiced.

HAIKU NOTEBOOKS

SPARROW NOTEBOOK (1995/1996)

after a rainstorm
sparrows are drawn
to the silver puddles

dry stones, wet stones
the eaves cast
a pale shadow

bending my head,
the fading scent
of rain-soaked peonies

rollerblades and sparrows
cut straight through
the late afternoon sunlight

autumn in the north:
a red maple leaf
floats downstream

late autumn sunlight
my urine—crystal clear
falling on the yellow leaves

first snow:
the eyes of the sparrows
sharp and bright

a morning below zero,
warmth rises
from the compost bucket

hey you sparrows!
I'm in my brown robe
where shall we go?

mid-winter thaw:
an icicle falls
beside the stray cat

my hot-water bottle
stone cold—
a long winter's night

down a narrow side-street
a garbage truck rattles
the old houses

a long plane flight:
I close my eyes somehow
missing out on spring

between the green trees
power-lines grow thicker
in the summer heat

sleeping lightly
with moonlight
on dogwood and clover

the roses appear
unreal in the twilight,
or perhaps it's me

my teacup cooling
on the windowsill,
dark leaves of the magnolia

this vanishing world:
watching fireflies
in a forest clearing

the two indoor cats
both turn their heads
towards the setting sun

first day of autumn,
pulling off its sock
the baby wriggles its toes

CLOUD NOTEBOOK (1997/1998)

strangely yellow –
an autumn maple
by lamplight

on the wharf
rusted bollards – blood red
in the setting sun

white butterflies
under the ragged edge
of a rain cloud

in full moonlight
wondering why
the snow doesn't melt

in the bag of almonds
a mouse has gnawed
an almond-sized hole

the hockey player
clears the snow off his car
with a hockey stick

frozen pavement
and a remote sky
strewn with clouds

winter's end—a wet
sandshoe, steam
from a manhole cover

spring sunlight:
in melted pond water
frogs are mating

the buzzing of a wasp
sharpened
by a cool breeze

ah, to be a cloud
moving slowly
above the cherry blossoms

pink shadows
on the footpath
beneath the cherry trees

unfocused heat—
I find myself
staring into the fan

unbroken heat—
the cicada's legs
are dry and brittle

right at the edge
of Niagara Falls
a starling catches moths

during the rainstorm
the child's colouring-in
becomes more intense

the sound of a river
rippling through
blue blue dragonflies

late autumn picnic:
a corner of the blanket
turned over by the wind

after my father's death
autumn leaves
the colour of whiskey

cold night,
she holds a pencil
between her teeth

SNOW NOTEBOOK (1999/2000)

fresh snow—
even the cigarette butts
sparkle

I stand amazed:
beyond the mounds of ice
a slow-moving freight train

bowing to the snowflakes
as they fall
on my fingertips

random calligraphy—
black twigs
in the snow

a heavy snowfall:
the dead in the cemetery
twice buried

receding snow:
the barber relaxes
in his barber's chair

winter's end –
a folded poem
stops the window rattling

lifting a cold stone
earthworms slowly withdraw
into their holes

the beginning of spring:
lifting another stone—
golden ants!

ascending the mountain
small toads
grow colder

twilight stream,
sound of a deer moving
through the long grass

summer thunder:
my capped tooth
begins to ache

reluctant rain,
the light withdraws
into dark green leaves

predawn to dawn:
as the day emerges
a crow caws

in the pale night sky
a giant tree
glistens with raindrops

old autumn dog
a yellow leaf
stuck to his back

each day less light,
the smell of printer's ink
on the morning newspaper

late autumn leaves
scattered across
a trampoline

after five days,
the body of a dead fly
still iridescent blue

a moonless night,
satellite dishes
half-filled with snow

FIREFLY NOTEBOOK (2001/2002)

first frost,
at midnight
a car alarm goes off

on the cutting board
the knife's shadow
sharp as the knife itself

the receding snow
releases a litter
of autumn leaves

the old broom
sweeps away
bits of itself

mid-winter thaw:
a squirrel and I
watch the icicles fall

cold night,
mice steal kapok
from my sitting cushion

hawk on a lamppost
first sunlight
gleaming in its eyes

in the big field
one snowflake falls …
then another

winter pier,
seagulls circle
an empty Ferris wheel

putting down his violin,
the waterfall
continues to play

light fading
from the magnolia blossoms—
she switches on the lamp

unsettled heart—
a crow keeps cawing
on the off-beat

reaching a dead end,
fireflies seen
through gaps in a fence

no frog,
but its wet shadow
left on a rock

deep in the forest
the shadow of ferns
on yellow mushrooms

on the hottest day
the faintest green
in a crow's feather

streams of minnows
moving moving
through clear water

abandoned tennis court,
faded balls decay
among the fallen leaves

red dragonflies
joined together
in the autumn wind

repairing a roof,
the golden leaves shine brighter
with each hammer blow

HAIBUN

WINTER AT CHAPIN MILL

no hand-slapping heat
of a tropical forest,
just ice-crystals
needle thin
falling on dry leaves

That afternoon, by the ruins of the railway bridge, the dog discovered the severed head of a deer lying on the ground. We made him walk ahead of us as the stench of decomposition was overwhelming. The dog, revered for his wise and affectionate nature, was obviously delighted. You could hear him panting with effort as he carried his prize before him, the deer's tongue lolling out from the side of its skull.

Sitting down for breakfast the next morning at a local diner, we listened to a nearby conversation. Two store-keepers were talking about guns, about which model had the best "knock down" power. The flesh on their faces was heavy, hanging down in folds, and the weight of their bodies gave the early-morning light, the pink upholstery, and the pale gray tables an unexpected seriousness.

because of the bare trees
with their spindly branches
I notice slats missing
in the old bench
by the edge of the pond

Winter opens everything up. From that hidden place, where once there issued only the voices of children and the slamming of doors, a house suddenly appears. And now that the foliage has been stripped away, the ridges of the hills are also exposed, revealing the precise musculature of the land with all its humps and hollows.

Gaps keep proliferating – between branches, between trees, between stones. On our way through the forest, there is not so much a silence that descends but a silence that deepens, broken only by the crunching of our boots as we walk across patches of frozen snow.

At night the far side of the pond is covered by a sheet of ice. We stand on the bank, by the watery blackness, and gaze towards this ghostly expanse of white. It floats in the void like a distant country. Like Norway. Like Siberia.

icicles hang
beside a wind chime,
fans of ice
overlap the edges
of a waterfall

The snow is stitched with animal tracks – small, blue indentations zigzagging over the fields. Near the gate, the split hoof-prints of a deer (easy to distinguish). Further up the path, the tracks of a rabbit, bunched together as it hopped across an open space. But what about those strange, trident-like marks, too wide apart to be a squirrel, too continuous to be a crow? It's as if a mysterious creature, a chimera, solidified in the cold air, pressed its feet into the whiteness while moving forward, then melted away into the shadows of the forest.

A mat of transparent ice adheres to the sides of a large rock. The rock rises from the middle of a gently flowing stream. Reflecting the snow-covered banks, the borders of the mat, suspended just above the surface, glisten white. When we gaze into the stream itself, we discover the forgotten green of water plants. A mythological, Grecian shade of green. The plants spread their tendrils and sway hypnotically in the slow pulse of the current.

on the feeding tray
a male cardinal
cracks sunflower seeds,
snowflakes falling
on his crimson feathers

A single flame perched on a bare branch, another cardinal calls from the edge of the forest. Behind him, on the snow-covered hillside, the thin trees and their shadows are evenly spaced between strips of light.

Passing through the forest, crossing the miniature stone bridge, we push open the basement door of an abandoned summer cottage. In the narrow, cobwebbed room, a circular mirror hangs above a battered chest of drawers. Its surface is clouded with patches of mold and speckled with dots of rust. In its depths, we find blurred images of ourselves, bundled up against the cold. This is a mirror reserved for moths and spiders, although no insects disturb its isolation during the long winter months. It remains a remote, forgotten mirror. A mirror of forgetting. A mirror of remoteness. And in our heavy coats we resemble two arctic explorers, near exhaustion, who peer into its glass as if into a cave of ice.

winter trees
still cold as steel,
unfolding between their roots
small green leaves
mottled with brown

The leaves are in camouflage. And in the absence of bright colours, the dirt-covered stone towers, which once supported the railway bridge, appear richly patterned. Beside the gravel path, the peeled wood of the power-poles glows a light pink. It's as if the timber were truly alive, as if a current of electricity flowed up the centre of each pole, and not through the thick wires hanging overhead.

We inhale the cool air, allowing it to fill our lungs. Our lives expand in the emptiness. Undefined clouds, without fibre or shading, stretch themselves across the pale sky.

Nothing issues from the cleft in the tree. Pressing my ear to its trunk, there is only silence. During the summer we watched an endless stream of bees flying in and out of this dark opening. Today they must be hibernating deep inside. Or perhaps they have perished in the cold. But no, such a life force can only be dormant. In early spring the trunk will vibrate again. Even now, when I close my eyes, along with the smell of resin I detect the faintest scent of honey.

in bare fields
stones materialize
above the melting snow
like bubbles released
from under the earth

At sunset a sudden wind comes from across a nearby field, blurring the trees and rattling the brambles. It's time to turn back. All of our journeys at Chapin Mill form one large circle, a going forth which becomes, by degrees, a returning. A walk along the periphery. A winter pilgrimage.

Several paces ahead, in the shade, the dog probes a stretch of unmelted snow, pressing his muzzle into the tracks of a deer. But the deer have gone. Nothing out of the ordinary remains to be encountered: neither an owl, nor a fox, nor a shaft of sunlight. The day is drawing to a close, and the dog leads us home.

IN TRANSIT

Rochester International Airport. In the spacious atrium between Concourse A and Concourse B, the authorities have placed fourteen old fashioned, cane rocking-chairs in a row, facing the large windows. Several people are seated in the chairs, rocking gently back and forth as they gaze across the snow-covered runway.

heat waves
from a turbojet
rippling the whiteness

Once we take off, there is no future and no past, just sunlight shimmering on the plane wing, a sea of clouds far below. I turn away from the window and look around the cabin. Half of the passengers are school children. A group of black, fourteen-year-old cheerleaders, dressed in identical track suits, sit together. When we touch down at Atlanta, Georgia, they give a spontaneous burst of applause.

low-pressure clouds:
in my neighbour's forehead
a vein pulsates

Ramada Inn, Los Angeles. In the grey light of early morning, standing on a balcony and surveying the passing traffic and dusty palm trees along West Century Boulevard, I find myself recalling Basho: 'The moon and sun are eternal travellers. Even the years wander on. A lifetime adrift in a boat, or in old age leading a tired horse … every day is a journey, and the journey itself is home.' In the background, an aerobics instructor tells her television audience, 'crack the egg between your shoulder-blades.'

simply to become
nothing but a shadow
cast by a dog
or a hedge
or a street sign

Los Angeles International Airport. Outside the Continental baggage claim area, two swarthy, Las Vegas-looking men are laughing and exchanging jokes. A stretch limousine pulls up and a middle-aged woman, with a mass of platinum hair and a tight dress, gets out and embraces the smaller of the men. A large black chauffeur stands by the car door as the three disappear into the tinted-glass interior. The chauffeur then produces a bottle of champagne, opens it with a flourish, and passes it inside. After that he folds himself into the driver's seat and the limousine slips away.

Honolulu International Airport. In a men's room cubicle, someone has carefully printed a line of Japanese characters down the narrow space between the wall tiles. A poem perhaps, or a wry observation on this tropical outpost of the United States. Whatever the message, I can't imagine anything obscene coming from such a delicate script.

in the Ala Wai canal
thin fish
with large eyes
glide
over Coca-Cola cans

Bach organ music is being piped through a crowded men's room on Concourse B of Chicago O'Hare Airport. In the midst of the coming and going, a blind Japanese man with a white cane stands by one of the washbasins. Having just washed his hands, he reaches into space and a stranger on his right passes him a paper towel. Having dried his hands, he turns his body to the left, with the slightest hesitation, and another stranger picks up his travel bag and hands it to him. These movements are performed with a transfixing, ballet-like precision. The Japanese man then gives a general 'Thank you', and exits into the stream of arriving and departing travellers.

Washington Dulles International Airport. Sitting at my departure gate, I look to see whether, by the remotest coincidence, there is someone I know among the multitude of people passing by. Once in a while I do catch a glimpse of a familiar mouth, a recognizable forehead, the stooped shoulders of someone from my past. But these are just fragments in the endless variety of faces and shapes that keep circulating. Everyone is unknown. However, in watching this continuous flow of existence, I can also acknowledge that all the tired, confused, concerned, alert, self-satisfied, forced, bemused, serene, and bewildered expressions are none other than my own; I have worn each of these expressions at one time or another.

Auckland International Airport's Chapel. Comments in the Visitors' Book:

Thanks Lord for a safe honeymoon trip.
Our lives are in your hands.
Our God is an awesome God.
Please help my sick grandfather and bless us on our holiday.
God bless the flight attendants.
Look after the people in Heaven.
Peace men party on.
Please don't let us crash.
I love my girlfriend.

And in the Arrivals area, the clear voice of a small girl, part song and part command: 'We have to watch for Aunty Meg and *all* her bags.'

Again I must depart from Auckland for the Northern Hemisphere. Sitting at a table in the airport cafeteria, I pick the last crumbs of pastry from my plate. In the background a rhythmic rumbling grows louder, and I imagine a group of Cook Island drummers farewelling their relatives. But the sound comes from a large plastic rubbish bin, which is slowly being wheeled through the food hall.

on the paper napkin
a rust-coloured stain
left by a tea-bag

Papeete Airport. The air is thick with the scent of frangipani. In a garden near the Transit Lounge, I sit among the roots of a banyan tree and listen to the Tahitian drummers greet another party of in-coming tourists. High above, in the midnight sky, the upper third of the moon has been diagonally cut away, transforming the remaining orb into the eye of a crocodile or a lizard. Just before landing in Tahiti an hour ago, on looking out the cabin window and catching sight of the southern constellations, I couldn't help but think, 'These are my stars.'

mesmerized by enormous
paddle-shaped leaves
and sharp red flowers

Landing at Chicago O'Hare Airport, in bright sunlight, the thousands of cars parked in the vast, mile-long parking lots are all sparkling like diamonds … . On the subterranean, neon-lit moving walkway, which links Concourse B and Concourse C, I look up at the mirrored ceiling and watch myself floating swiftly by on the dark, metallic surface.

from the very beginning
a disembodied voice
tells you that
'the moving walkway
is now ending'

Transient. In transit. Intransigent. My perceptions are always sharpened when I'm about to leave one place, or have just arrived in another. But in the course of a long flight, they become dull and blunt. I find myself reduced to word play, to filling out the crossword puzzle in the back of the airline's magazine. Only when I can gaze out the cabin window does the world return with its depth and clarity.

a cloud skull
isolated above
the taut
blue skin
of the ocean

Rochester International Airport. In the early morning the terminal is nearly deserted. The few people waiting at their departure gates are very still, as if they are in an Edward Hopper painting, surrounded by rows of vacant seats and back-lit by long banks of windows. Down on the tarmac the chains of baggage carts remain motionless. Each cart has its heavy plastic curtain drawn back to reveal a small, dark stage. But there is no performance to be enacted, and no one to make an exit or entrance. Overhead, the concertinaed ends of the jetways hang empty in mid-air.

first snowflakes
falling
on silver metal

At a local park, I pat a shaggy Labrador and feel ice crystals clinging to the tips of his fur. It's been ten months since I returned to Rochester, and we're now well into winter. When I walk down the street and catch sight of a plane passing through the sky, I think to myself, 'Yes, it's almost time to leave', or 'One more week and I'll be gone.'

MILDNESS

The Fan

switching on the fan
white waves rise and fall
far out at sea

In the front garden, an early summer wind rotates the taro leaves. Drawn towards a green centre, you hear a humming that could be from an insect, but is in fact the sound of green itself, the first faint note of a song which will unfold in the weeks to come. Already the heat has made you uncomfortable, like a heavy garment hanging from your shoulders. With a languid movement, your left hand turns on the fan as you stare out to sea—a sea that belongs to another season with its stark and uncompromising waves.

as the day heats up
fruit-flies settle
on the kitchen sponge

Summer seems to have been here forever, uninterrupted and complete. The small insects take a break from the metal bucket under the sink, that container filled with still-life: lettuce leaves, egg shells, the scooped out halves of grapefruit and avocados, the rinds of oranges and watermelons, the skins of bananas . . . yellow flecked with black, pink fading into white, brown pressed against purple … . The process of decay emits a strong and musty odour. I know that I should take the bucket outside and tip its contents into the compost bin, but I linger by the bench, observing two fruit-flies who have summoned up the energy to mate. As the male mounts the female, their eyes appear like dots of blood.

The Motorway

a strong wind after midnight:
hibiscus flowers scattered
on the motorway on-ramp

You slow down to avoid crushing the flowers. Perhaps the sides of your tyres are brushed with pollen. This thought makes you smile. In the darkness of your heart a space opens. An aperture. The lanes of the motorway are glistening after a shower of rain. You wind down your window to breathe in the night air, and the lights of the city pass overhead. Bright, clear threads of neon. They bind you to nothing. They glide over the bodywork of your car, then slip away as you follow the curve of the harbour and the silent expanse of ocean.

slowly, over the years,
the dead leave you;
they have other concerns
they now see the world
through different eyes
and you are truly alone

When I drive over this section of road, especially at night, I often think of my mother, who died a decade ago. Then I was heading towards the city and the brightly-lit interior of a hospital; now I am driving away, a stranger to a loved one (no longer a presence but only a memory), and also a stranger to the city itself, which has changed so much in ten years. But this is perhaps the way it should be. The rain comes down again, and I let the drops accumulate on the windscreen. It's like I'm travelling under water; I could be on a remote stretch of road at the bottom of the sea.

The Telephone

a warm evening:
the wing-beats of a blackbird
fade across the lawn

I'm waiting for the telephone to ring. It's a cordless phone, curved like a large and elongated ear. I have a faint ringing in my own ears. When I pick up the phone, I hear my voice, my inner voice. It says what I know already; no one is there. How long has there been no one there? All day long. From day tip to night tip. From the tips of my toes to the top of my head. I hold the telephone at arm's length and study the pattern of small holes in the centre of the ear-piece. Listen … voices of children can be heard in the distance; and outside my window, the rustling of a blackbird as it searches for insects beneath a hedge.

answer me
or at least
ask me a question
that I can answer

In the old house someone runs down a long wooden staircase. Their heavy shoes make the boards creak and the nails vibrate (nails which have been in the wood for a hundred years). You're so sensitive to noise. You would like to be ancient, and callused, and as unaware as a chunk of granite. And yet your ears never cease receiving sounds. More and more you're flooded with life; a filter for neutrinos (those smallest of subatomic particles); a silk-screen for a myriad of different sensations (some of them red, some of them blue). Just as the footsteps reach the ground floor, the telephone stops ringing.

The Mirror

full moon
in the blue sky:
a lingering
circle of chalk

The mirror stand dissolves and the mirror floats away. He lives on the moon but has designs on the earth. Against the backdrop of a familiar crater, he imagines the shimmering leaves of a gingko tree (if any tree were to grow on the moon, it would be a gingko). With life reflected far above, in the vastness of space, he recalls how he once posted a letter, tended a garden, swam in the ocean. But this was before he lost his kingdom, before the jewels bled from his crown. Now he has only earth-light, and silence, and a broken comb to run through his hair.

skeins of red silk—
the sirens
of ambulances
and fire engines

I sit facing the wall. Above my head hangs a round mirror, not a convex one like the Flemish masters loved to place in their paintings—a swelling of glass that contained the entire room as well as the outside world—but a round mirror nonetheless. In its depths, undistorted, lie the subdued light and the shadows of my apartment. But I stay where I am, unwilling to stand up in case I catch a glimpse of myself in the mirror. As if in a dream, I may have aged overnight; all my teeth may be missing; I may have begun to resemble someone I detest. Then there is the opposite: the fear of finding myself completely unchanged.

The Armchair

curled up
the cat is always
at the centre
of herself

This morning I woke up struggling, just as the previous night I had gone to bed fighting with myself. For a week now it's been a constant battle. Everything has become easy—that's where the difficulty lies. Whatever I touch is pliant, unresisting, intrinsically soft—that's the hardest part. So, at least for today, I refuse to relax in my favorite armchair, an action that would be tantamount to dropping my guard. What I must do is maintain the pressure, moment by moment asking the same questions: Who am I? What have I done? What am I to do now? … I don't know, and my mildness—which makes me accept any situation—is slowly driving me wild.

a dense cloud
of cigar smoke
drifts towards the hedge

Dust-brown sparrows chirp in the background; a scrap of yellowed cellophane vibrates on the pavement; a swollen and murky sun makes a brief appearance beneath a layer of clouds. Its light catches a golden chain, worn by the man in an open-necked shirt who is sitting in an armchair on the front porch of his clapboard house. He's been there all afternoon, smoking a series of cigars and watching the street, boredom etched on his face. No doubt he's a hit-man by profession. A killer of time. And just because his inertia exerts a certain fascination, you find it necessary to avert your gaze.

The Shower

on the hottest day
when you hear someone
taking a shower
you think to yourself
'Ah, that feels good!'

A narrow stream flows between the shoulder-blades, into the small of the back, over the curve of the buttocks, droplets clinging to the warm skin as the body slowly turns into the full force of the water. Sometimes it's as though only one form exists, only one sensation. At other times you're pierced by your aloneness; you long to merge with another person, to liquefy. The gap that you feel—between losing your own boundaries and being painfully aware of them—is also your passageway from one moment to the next. You take a deep breath. The water continues to fall. You take another deep breath.

bubbling up
the horse chestnut's
bright green leaves

Down on the earth I'm bathed in green, swathed and swaddled in the comfort of trees. And when evening comes, after a shower of rain, I discover a colony of ornate snails in the back garden, their shells made from miniature panels of inlaid wood. The snails are gliding over wet stones, while deeper in the shadows, among the twigs and fallen leaves, pale mushrooms have materialized through a layer of mulch. I study their white domes, and, from underneath, the soft compacting of brown ridges (for I have become very small, hardly more than a cloud of awareness that condenses then departs).

The Mist

a golden light
in the rear-vision mirror
as the sun rises
through early morning mist

The stark cliffs are in the background, invisible along with the margin of white sand and the pale gray of the ocean. Ten minutes ago she watched the mist roll between the dunes. Now it has enveloped her car, pressing its opaqueness against the windows … . Oyster-catchers, dotterels, terns, shags, black-backed gulls—they're all close at hand, and yet she can't see them. A pair of binoculars lies on the passenger seat beside a badly-folded map. A membrane of roads to go with a membrane of thoughts. She feels frail at being undecided, uncertain of her future as the mist recedes. Then, with a fierceness that surprises her, she pulls off her wedding ring and shuts it in the glove box.

frost on the power-lines:
strands of silver strung
from pole to pole

It's as if a giant spider has been at work. Driving along a gravel road, stones ricochet off the undercarriage of my car. In a field, a calf drinks rainwater from a sheet of corrugated iron. On a hillside, the headstones of an old cemetery catch the sunlight and shine like rows of teeth … . The road continues in a series of twists and turns, and I continue, isolated yet coexistent with every single thing: with the sun, with the remaining patches of mist, with a hawk that takes flight from the side of the road. For a brief moment, as the hawk rises into the sky, its talons are fully extended beneath its muscular legs.

The Study

everything corresponds
from a pencil sharpener
to a passing comet

The cat is lying in a rectangle of sunlight. When a fly lands beside her on the carpet, she flicks out a paw. The fly escapes into another room, and the cat closes her eyes. I witness this minor drama from my armchair. Then, putting aside my book, I enter the study, sit down at my desk, and write about what I've just observed. It's not much, but at that precise point in time and space it was everything. And the sitting-down-at-my-desk and the taking-up-of-my-pen form their own totality. The exact weight of the moment; a counterbalance to those long periods, so easily forgotten, in which I had nothing to relate.

the inside is not so different
from the outside:
a movement of your bowels
and then the passing clouds

Wandering through a pet shop, you stop by a large aquarium. Even without a tube of light, the water appears fluorescent as the tank stands against a wall that's been painted a vivid blue. You take your time and observe the large goldfish, especially one who lies motionless at the bottom of the tank, his fins splayed out on a layer of pink gravel. The goldfish stares fixedly into a clump of reeds as though deep in meditation. Then again, he could be on the point of dying. You wait for several minutes until a slight movement of his gills suggests that he's more or less alive. Alive to what? You look around and see a pale reflection of yourself in the front window, along with the fish tanks, and the dog baskets, and the bird-cages.

The Eclipse

nobody thinks
about banding
the thin legs
of the sparrows

They sharpen their beaks on the backs of the chairs and hop onto my table, expecting me to share some of my sandwiches. 'Are ye not of more worth than many sparrows?' 'No,' I would have to respond as one flies away with a bit of crust. 'Even a single sparrow, at this moment, is my equal.' Beyond the café terrace, the surface of the harbour is a calm and solemn gray. The storm, which has just passed, has taken away the light as well as the rain so that everything is now subdued, except for the small birds. And even though my mood tends towards the melancholic, I can't help but smile, knowing that I can never be completely alone when in the company of sparrows.

thunder without clouds
space without time
wind without the earth

The shadows of trees soften, with crescent shapes swirling like bubbles among the blurred outlines of leaves. Overhead, the sky is a remote blue, although possessing a peculiar density so that it appears, not like the interior of a dome, but like the outer surface of a gigantic sphere. People fall silent as they move across the lawn, engrossed in the subtle diffusion of light. One group of friends remains standing beside their picnic blanket. They take turns holding up a dark rectangle of glass. Through the smoky lens, the black ball of the moon can be seen blocking the sun, with only a thin halo of the brightest green visible around the edge.

The Window

the late afternoon
sunlight
folds itself
down the stairs

It's an unpredictable time of day, a time of apparent calm when someone could just step outside and keep walking through the evening and into the night .... Inside the dining room, a slight breeze parts the curtains. The lower half of your body is lost from view as you sit at the table near the window, leaning on your forearms. The table is solid and prevents you from moving forward; it acts as a barrier, a check to any impulse you might have to open the front door and disappear. Of course, you could push aside your chair and stand up, but the deliberateness of such an action would be inappropriate, especially as everything is so finely balanced .... One thought replaces another. The fading light gives you a little extra weight.

late night reading:
an eyelash falls
onto the page

In the morning I awake to the smell of freshly-sharpened pencils. Lying back in bed, I listen to the breeze rustling the sheets of blank paper that lie in a pile on my desk. In a few hours my third floor room will become unbearably hot. I should get a fan—that would be the sensible thing to do. But for the moment I decide simply to write about a fan, or to begin writing with the image of a fan and then proceed to the ocean. Beyond my window, there is only a large and vacant carpark. To reach the nearest ocean would take at least a day by car. However, when I close my eyes, I can hear the sound of the waves.

TANKA SEQUENCES

GATHERING CLOUDS

1.

cars accelerate past
our sitting for peace,
a cool breeze brings us
the shadow of pigeons
the smell of hotdogs

end of summer—
the soft tar now hard,
a cigar butt
stands upright
on the sidewalk

under concrete towers
people talk of chest pains
and the approaching war,
tips of the oak leaves
begin to turn yellow

as the car window
closes
electronically
his face disappears
in a flash of light

2.

"Iraq Admits
Weapons Inspectors"
so far away and yet
the sunflowers here
are also fading

outside the entrance
to the funeral home
a broken beer bottle,
I think of a dark ship
launched into the darkness

downtown abandoned
the only people
those who wait for buses,
I ask myself
has a bomb fallen somewhere?

in the middle
of nowhere, a forlorn
orphaned garden
dedicated to
ten sister cities

3.

the sunlight
now cold,
red berries
falling
from the dogwood tree

"U.S. Will Not Go To War
With The Iraqi People"
a squirrel holds its chestnut
as if looking into
a crystal ball

outside the grim
apartment building
a pack of playing cards;
kings and queens
scattered among the bushes

every ladder I see
is either crooked
or broken,
and every person
overweight

4.

buying a small, black skull
from the Mexican shop
I glide past
my own dark thoughts
this autumn evening

marigolds growing
in a vacant lot,
and a Dead End sign
with a sticker that says
"It's Okay"

throughout the day
a foreboding of
unwholesome karma
ripening in this land
of bright opportunity

a fire engine moves slowly
down a green corridor
no heat no rain,
the black skull smiles
in the palm of my hand

5.

the sun beaming down
on satellite dishes,
near the edge of the road
rows of pumpkins
waiting to be carved

"Blast Cripples French Tanker"
the door to the diner
propped open with a cinder block,
people hurry by
dressed in winter clothes

nodding to the same man
I passed yesterday,
so few of us
prowling the streets
of this empty city

Bush talks about not waiting
for a mushroom cloud,
in the window
of the Japanese restaurant
sun-faded displays of sushi

6.

defining the edges
of lawns and sidewalks,
golden locust leaves
darkened
by the heavy rain

a fall in pressure
and my head throbs,
a thin concrete line
circling the reservoir
separates water from sky

all of one colour
the light in men's eyes
am I walking among ghosts?
leaves scuttle across the road
pigeons peck the dust

through the tavern's
tinted windows
a white ball
on the pool table
shines like the moon

7.

carrying a book on Grünewald
along the empty streets,
his hummingbird angels
and hybrid demons
give life to my inner world

bombs explode in distant lands,
blackened fire-escapes,
chimneys releasing
white smoke
into a white sky

left at the bus stop,
a small pile
of children's books
tied together
with black ribbon

inside the Halloween store
severed heads in jars,
outside a chorus
of crows crying, crying
through the skeletal trees

8.

"Republicans Take Senate"
the distorted reflections
of mirrored buildings
for a moment more real
than the buildings themselves

Midtown Bus Terminal:
people drink coffee
and smoke their cigarettes
as if it were
the last day on earth

these small bushes
with burning
orange leaves,
the wind has yet
to tear them away

Friday evening,
everything speeds up
even the sun
going down

WINTER SHADOWS

1.

by the frozen pond
overturned dinghies
laid out like
metal coffins
in the snow

silent farmland,
between strips of snow
desolate corn stubble
golden
in the afternoon light

on the dirt road
around each puddle
a silver perimeter,
and my mind
part mud, part crystal

as if to acknowledge
this big red barn,
the blast
of a train whistle
somewhere in the background

on Thanksgiving Day
finding the tracks
of wild turkeys
I feel grateful
for all living things

a distant memory
of my dead parents,
a deer emerges
from the forest
at twilight

2.

shoveling snow
into the stream
without a thought,
dull grey clouds
glide away

snowflakes falling
on my lips,
no sound comes
from the outside
or from within

No Trespassing
the sign – so yellow,
I could expire
in this land
without boundaries

snow flowing
like sand,
the skeletal trees
sway
in the wind

following the footprints
of a hunter
who follows a deer trail
deeper, deeper
into the forest

ice falls from branches
at my approach,
I'm not a ghost—
that much I know
as the light fades

3.

wild turkeys take flight
at the edge
of a white field,
left behind –
the imprint of their wings

in the snow-covered quarry
the hills of gravel
are hibernating,
this wanderer passes
as if in a dream

how long a life
do these icicles have?
drop by drop
I am leaving
the colours of winter

at 30,000 feet
the clouds form
a vast field of snow,
I cast no shadow
so far from earth

BARRIER CROSSINGS

1.

cooking my porridge
at dawn
I feel aligned with
those ancient
Chinese hermits

seated on a tree stump
at my stone table,
cold in the morning
still cold
in the afternoon

admitting that I have
nothing more to write,
I receive
the voices of tuis
the pulse of the river

a green haze
deep in the valley,
when I finish my paragraph
the wind tells me
it's time to turn the page

2.

pohutukawas
at Rosalie Bay –
difficult to tell
where the trees end
and the stones begin

a mosquito
even on this
remote rock,
is it aware
of the crashing surf?

although I'm warmed
by the winter sunlight
the desolate cliffs
behind me
remain in the shade

white driftwood
on a pebbled beach,
I listen to the rocks
being ground together
beneath the waves

3.

on the anniversary
of Hillary's
climbing of Everest
I struggle up a slope
of ferns and manuka

high on the ridge
cellular calls break up,
the faint voice
of the one I love
dissolving into space

keeping my balance
down a trail
of yellow clay,
at this moment
this is my life

dog at the top
of the long descent
dog at the bottom
both barking
barking

4.

venerable puriri,
elephant-eyed
digging massive
blunt-toed roots
into the dark earth

venerable puriri,
your trunk puckered
with anus-like hollows—
an ancient pillar
of earthiness

venerable puriri,
lashed to the forest floor
with rata vines,
fountains of epiphytes
cascade from your branches

venerable puriri,
having tied yourself in knots
to sustain your great weight
you now lean for support
against the sky

5.

walking down
the gravel road
by Kaitoke Swamp,
no traffic
just the buzzing of flies

sometimes I think
that I'm only alive
when I walk—
but I have this thought
while walking

the hot springs
now cool,
a cloud of midges
hovers
above my towel

through the reeds
a wooden walkway
the trees like sentinels,
no one comes
no one goes

6.

caught in a downpour
I take shelter
in an abandoned car,
pine needles scattered
across the dashboard

at Blind Bay
inhaling
the smell of seaweed,
I peel off
my damp clothes

concrete terraces—
all that is left
of the whaling station,
a man welds steel plates
to the hull of his boat

old iron moorings
flaking away
revealing their sinews,
grey clouds gather
above the mountains

7.

Awana
by the pines
is one of those places
I may revisit
after I'm gone

the same white horse
I photographed
ten years ago
standing in the same field
so very still

white picket fences
around the graves
of those who died at sea,
below the waves break
along a deserted beach

at the thin waterfall
it begins to rain,
a native rat
darts away
beneath the ferns

8.

fern-dark passage
a chill rising
from the stones,
the light of the sun
is more like the moon

fantails
the slanting rays
of winter sunlight
and my own
disjointed thoughts

the sound of
dead palm fronds
scraping on the ground,
the northeast wind
is dry and cold

the more I linger
on this trail
the more it will tell me,
another time – I whisper
another time

Tanka Sequence notes:

Gathering Clouds written between mid-September and mid-November, 2002, in Rochester, upstate New York, during a period when the Bush Administration was intensifying its preparations for war against Iraq.

Winter Shadows written at Chapin Mill, the Rochester Zen Center's country land in upstate New York, during late November and December, 2002, before I returned to live in New Zealand.

Barrier Crossings written at Little Goat on Great Barrier Island from mid-May to the beginning of July, 2003.

PROSE

DREAMS

As the sun slips below the horizon, a swan closes its eyes

At a Chinese restaurant, a Chinese waiter eats his evening meal
with a knife and fork

A woman drops her child on the carpet, and instead of crying it
laughs

In the car-wrecker's yard, fragments of window glass sparkle in the
sunlight

A strip of red balloon hangs from the beak of a seagull

*

After a fight at school, acorns are found on the toilet floor

At the edge of a storm, someone is heard sweeping leaves

In the back garden, rain drips from the eaves of a doll's house

The sunset glows pink inside the ears of a black dog

In a takeaway bar, a machine for killing flies is switched on

*

A man holds a bicycle wheel and walks into a cathedral

In the middle of summer, a band-aid has melted on the asphalt

A wooden swan sits in a bakery, its back hollowed out and filled with loaves of bread

A wasp picks up a single grain of rice, disappears, then returns to pick up another grain

The dark clouds are darker through the skylight of a limousine

*

When its master blows down a cardboard tube, the dog cocks its head to one side

A wire coat-hanger is found lying in the snow, and later on, a slice of white bread

A man sells oranges in front of an empty field that stretches towards the horizon

On the beach at night, as the fire dies down, the sound of the ocean increases

*

A jogger runs past with *Stop Acid Rain* printed on his tee-shirt

In the crowded men's room, all three toilet doors change from "occupied" to "vacant" at the same time

At a serious accident, an ambulance arrives before the tow trucks

The letters on a tomato sign are the same red as the tomatoes

When the corn field is harvested, the hedgerows rustle with mice

*

At the airport, baggage tickets hang from the circular light above the check-in desk

A steel girder casts its shadow across the side of a concrete building

A gust of wind sends the cellophane from a cigarette packet high up into the evening sky

On a late-night bus, an old man smelling of beer manages to complete a crossword puzzle

A cat slips between two candles without singeing its tail

*

Cleaning under his bed, a writer finds his lost pen covered in dust

In the archeological museum, a series of crystalline *pings* are heard when the lights are switched on

Two painters in white overalls each stand on a white ladder and paint the same building white

In the Japanese garden, a carp with a human face glides by

On a corrugated iron roof, a seagull opens and closes its beak

*

A pile of cigarette butts lies at the end of a long pier

In a house by the sea, a man in his night-shirt is changing a light-bulb

In the hair salon, a small girl places two red plastic straws in her hair

An empty cassette box shines like a pool of water on a dark bedspread

The shadow of a cat sits on the shadow of a fence

*

Outside a tropical hotel, a hotel worker is struck by a large leaf

A young mother drives around the block until her babies are fast asleep

A chandelier of icicles hangs from the underside of a rusted fire-escape

Light shines through a blowfly as it settles on a television screen

Lotuses are opening beneath high-tension wires

*

An ice-cream van breaks down right beside a waterfall

A dog barks, and snow falls from a tree

REALITIES

Early spring: unaware that the old house has been sold to a developer, the starlings continue to make their nest under the eaves of the roof.

*

Pure happiness is fleeting, as when you make a pun or a joke in a dream and think it's extremely funny, only to realize, on waking up and recalling the dream, that your witticism is in fact rather childish, or completely incomprehensible.

*

They talk about "The Great Way", or "The Royal Way", but long ago it was just a simple path, overgrown with weeds, and night had fallen, and you were lost.

*

Auden says, 'Beams from your car may cross a bedroom wall', the light, segmented by Venetian blinds, forming a fluid zebra crossing, while the sleep-walker, that unconscious pedestrian of the early hours, remains safe in bed, his feet moving beneath the sheets as if he were passing through the air.

*

On the other side of the world, on the door of a fridge, there is also a photograph of a small dog who sits on the kitchen floor and looks up into the eye of the camera.

*

What do we record if not those moments that keep slipping away: the play of light on a body of water; the one who makes light of herself, with a shawl, with a scarf; the crack in a pane of glass, glowing like a vein of blood as the sun sets in mid-winter.

*

While pouring sand out of the eye-sockets of a skull, the lonely giant hears the percussive sound of a large goose running across a bamboo bridge.

*

Sometimes I think that dogs have an awareness, however vague, that they will die, and therefore let out a sigh every now and then; whereas cats, who are so self-contained, have already returned from the dead, and just sit there, suffused with a strange understanding.

*

Someone you have always loved is in love again, but with another person, and you are free to stand out of their circle and watch them spin in the midst of a fine rain, a rain that drifts towards you, mingled with the sweetness of their breath.

*

His left shoulder-blade twitched as if a wing were growing from inside the bone, and he realized, perhaps for the first time, that the horns he had secretly worn were in fact a half-formed halo.

*

A little bird, chirping outside my window, covers this bare tree in red flowers, and I sigh, and the sigh remains like a faint star in the twilight of my room.

*

He wanted to paint the crucifixion from behind, but when he imagined the scene, the back of the cross began to recede as the surrounding landscape spread out, the hill of Golgotha leading him down to a stony plain, and then to a river beside which there stood a small thatched cottage.

*

At the end of the world, on a deserted beach, a young god has been transformed into three circles of cut glass, the size of headlights, which lie embedded in a long plank of driftwood.

*

He wrote, 'I wish to be able to live my life without metaphors,' and then he added, 'like a fish swimming through clear water.'

*

Another winter spent in a northern land: looking at the icicles that lengthen beneath the eaves of the houses, I can't help but think, 'I'm getting long in the tooth.'

*

When we've gone, the wind will lean against a lamp-post; and the solitary heron, who usually walks beside the water's edge, will take up a piece of seaweed and fly into the branches of a pine tree.

MYTHS

I'm naked cleaning the inside of the bath. Moonlight shines through the window. I'm cleaning with the moonlight. With a white sponge. I'm taking a bath on the moon.

Distracted by a sphinx moth, the red cliffs have faded. The moth vibrates like a hummingbird. The cliffs also vibrate. And the sun climbs a cactus, spine by spine.

Cat wrestling a doormat with a storm in the background. Sketch the cat, before the storm comes, before the doormat is unravelled. The black storm, clawed and torn apart.

Bodies like dreams in action, bodies like images in a mirror. Flickering, freed from their attachments. In this twilight forest of transformations, I will become dark and paper thin.

Light shines under the arch of her foot. A soft, warm light. She leans against a pillar. Silent in the darkness. Read to me. She is reading my thoughts.

There are mountains inside of mountains. Steep and muscular, with ridges and hollows. Emerging at night, receding at dawn. They leave behind charcoal-black cows and bone-white sheep.

The sea wears my face as a mask. A thin disguise, for I am mostly water. And my ears, floating close to the surface, hear nothing but the waves.

Strange letters of light play on the ceiling, illegible yet meaning something. Fading when a cloud passes across the sun, then reappearing. Elusive letters of light from the heavens.

A young woman, seated on the front steps of a run-down apartment building, silently holds her cell phone before her as if she were looking into a mirror.

The oracle clearly told me, 'Remember who you were meant to become.' But what if I can't remember? And what if I don't want to become anything at all?

The pine trees sway with the weight of stars. Cobwebs gleam between their needles. The stars have come down like spiders. Spinning, spinning their threads as the earth turns.

Now I am Aeipolos, the ever-rotating one. When I keep myself in motion, nothing adheres to me. Shining a clear light, I enter a land of lotus fibres.

Even the wind sounds like the rain. The ogre coming in and the ogre going out can't recognize each other. The rain has aged them and rusted their battleaxes.

Octopus angel, ascending the walls of her aquarium, tentacles flowing from her centre, gently caressing the glass. She announces that everything is far more mysterious than we had imagined.

Coloured cities floating by in a grey mist. How can these things be? And yet they are. With spires and minarets. Coloured cities floating by in a grey mist.

Skeletons seen between the trees. Tons of skeletons, unearthed by front-end loaders. Unknown and unloved. I will cover their bones. I will cover their bones then go underground.

An enormous mastiff stands alone inside the laundromat, surrounded by washing machines and spin-driers. He is guarding the clothes of the dead. No one passes through this town.

After the goddess left the beach, I placed my bare feet in each set of her footprints, believing that a little of her warmth still remained in the sand.

REFLECTIONS

After buzzing around the room for five minutes, the blowfly exits through the open door, into the vast outside. I remain behind, contained within a small box of thoughts and feelings.

*

On the front porch, grapevines hang from the pergola and entwine themselves through the trelliswork. Overripe at the end of summer, the grapes are punctured by tiny birds - waxeyes - and probed by swarms of bees. My own skin is splitting open, slowly, while the vine leaves turn yellow and rustle in the wind. When storm clouds gather above the hills, the bunches of grapes darken.

*

The baaing of sheep in a nearby field sounds too perfect, too well-orchestrated. The sheep are pretending to be sheep. I write this observation down in my notebook, as though it were evidence of a conspiracy directed against me. Only when they fall silent do I forget about them, and the sheep become sheep again.

*

A car can be heard driving over gravel. As the sound of its engine diminishes, I relax. The house is hidden from the road by a stand of macrocarpas, their lower branches and leaves pale with dust. And I have faded from the world, for a few weeks at least. My fingers touch the keys of a typewriter. Evening draws closer. In a corner of the room, a spider spins its web.

*

The candle flame flickers as a sudden wind moves around the house. A minute later, a downpour of rain strikes the corrugated roof and darkens the front deck. Then everything becomes still. I put on a tape of sad Portuguese music. While the flame remains perfectly vertical, tapering to a knife-point of incandescent orange, a distant accordion presses itself gently against my chest.

*

At midnight, the wet road gleams like pewter. Potholes are filled with milky water, their surfaces too opaque to reflect the full moon. Looking up, the moon itself is now hidden behind a layer of clouds. Black trees, in silhouette, form a ragged corridor that recedes towards the smoke-grey hills. I would like a mist to arise and envelope me. But it's too warm. And as the clouds draw apart, the moon spotlights my solitary figure standing in the middle of the road.

*

A ceaseless, slender, subtropical rain continues to fall. I let in a ginger cat who is yowling at the back door. She nervously enters the house, lifting her front paw like a squirrel as she looks around. Yesterday I thought a blue jay flew past the window (it turned out to be a kingfisher). Although I'm north of Auckland, I still get flashes of upstate New York. But the rain here is nothing like the snow I left behind; it creates a green light, blurring the trees and softening the grass.

*

I imagine us lying on a soft bed of toetoe fronds, shaded by poplars, their upper branches swaying in the breeze. I brush your hair from your forehead. Our bodies are sheathed in white flames … . This reverie ends with the beating of wings; a woodpigeon has landed on the small magnolia tree in the garden. The bruised pods are beginning to break open, and the pigeon gulps down their bright red seeds.

*

After a day of rain, everywhere I look mosquitoes are mating: on the walls, on the ceiling, on the desk, on my pile of typing paper. They continue uninterrupted as I draw nearer to inspect them. On the front deck a dying bee, unable to fly, is cleaning its feelers. A female sparrow lands a few feet away, excited, holding a green cicada in her beak. This afternoon I'm surrounded by sparks of life and death, pinpoints of an energy that intensifies at the beginning of autumn.

*

Performing arabesques in mid-air, a fantail catches midges above the compost heap. In an upper field, the trunk of a large tree lies blackened and shattered, clods of earth still clinging to its roots. I take up and put down my pen. It's a day of heaviness and lightness. As a diversion, I decide to go outdoors and pick a few lemons. Like a reminder of something that I've forgotten, a damp tea towel hangs from the washing line.

*

The writing project that I am working on – a eulogy to my father – is taking shape. But the more I recall the past, the more mysterious the present becomes. Footsteps rattle across the ceiling, followed by a thud outside my window. A possum. A heartbeat. Once again I walk into the darkness. As the road dips downward, stars shine under the telephone wires.

ESSAYS

WORKING WITH NAGARJUNA

half a glass of wine
and I can't read
a word of Nagarjuna

In a Los Angeles Airport bookstore, I recently picked up a copy of *Verses from the Center*, Stephen Batchelor's radiant translation of Nagarjuna's principal work.

Nagarjuna, a visionary monk who lived in India during the second century, wrote *Verses from the Center* as a free-wheeling meditation on the Buddhist teaching of emptiness. This emptiness is not perceived as a gaping void, but as a way to liberation, a wonderful solvent that unglues us from fixed concepts such as "me" and "you", "self" and "other".

Nagarjuna's writing is elusive and precise, challenging and ambiguous. He uses words to go beyond words, to lever open spaces that have been sealed shut by rational thought. In this respect he is a great poet as well as a revolutionary thinker. At times playful and creative, he pushes the reader into unfamiliar territory, calling for an intuitive response to his flashes of insight and provocative questions.

In his introduction to *Verses from the Center,* Stephen Batchelor notes that 'The seeds of Nagarjuna's verses have borne and continue to bear fruit.' *Working with Nagarjuna* is my own response to a selection of these verses. My sections of prose form a series of small eddies, each of which has been stirred up by Nagarjuna's probing.

*

These moving feet reveal a walker
But did not start him on his way.
There was no walker prior to departure.
Who was going where?

Up ahead the dirt road curves around the bend. I am walking through the early evening. I've never been on this particular road, and yet it's the same road that stretched before me in Sardinia, and in Mexico, and in Spain. All the back roads of my past are continuous, and I walk over their cracked surfaces as the light begins to fade. Near the end of his life, Samuel Beckett wrote that he was on his 'last crooked straight'. I have a way to go … . Is that the sound of the ocean or the wind through the trees? It doesn't matter. There will always be a figure in a landscape—someone moving slowly along a path.

Seeing reveals a seer,
Who is neither detached
Nor undetached from seeing.
How could you see,
And what would you see
In the absence of a seer?

Light ripples across the leaves of a willow, in ever-widening circles, as you enter the pond. Take away all that you have seen—all the ugliness and the brutality and the suffering. Erase each painful moment, and you will erase yourself. Better to shine a light through these eyes, to become clear in water and in fire … . The world is passing through you. Blink, and it's gone. Blink, and it begins again.

I have no body apart
From parts which form it;
I know no parts
Apart from a "body".

On a remote beach, the wind is so powerful that people tie their bags to a thick pole embedded in the sand. The only shelter is to be found among the waves. But they appear to be breaking on the horizon, and as my legs are tired, I kneel down in a hollow between the dunes. Lowering my eyes, I watch millions of grains flowing past. Blasted by the wind, the grains of my flesh could also flow away. In the flux, there can be no body that holds my different parts together, no central post to which they could adhere. And yet I remain where I am. Increasingly encrusted. The sky glows white in the late afternoon.

What do you think
Of a freedom that never happens?
What do you make
Of a life that won't go away?

On the kitchen windowsill, a blue plastic cup, filled to the brim with cicada shells. She tried to sleep herself into exhaustion, but she kept waking up. After a week of daytime television, she wanted to sew herself into a cocoon, although she knew that no transformation would take place: she would remain herself, and her life would continue to be her life. This is when she started to fill the cup with shells. Each cicada had cracked the hump of its back to emerge as … a cicada. Nothing more and nothing less. Hundreds were singing around her house; they had stitched together the summer. And she realized that if she stopped fixating on herself, she would simply become a part of their song.

Isn't the appearance
And disappearance
Of seeds and fruits
The flow of life itself?

The grapes are darker when the sun shines through the vine leaves. Heavy, purple clusters hang above the front verandah. Today I'm drawn outside by the chattering of a fantail. It flits from vine to vine, knocking mosquitoes off the leaves before catching them in mid-air. Clever little bird. When the sun passes behind a cloud, the leaves change from bright green to yellow. On his album, *Another Green World*, Brian Eno sings, 'putting grapes back on the vine'. But the grapes have always been there. And the fantails, and the mosquitoes … . The verandah turns into the prow of a ship and ploughs its way through the long grass.

Buddhanature
Is the nature of this world.
Buddhanature has no nature
Nor does this world.

The receding tide leaves streaks of foam along the sand. The small bubbles, in their clusters, are rainbow-hued, each one like a miniature piece of stained glass. But the colours will soon vanish in the heat of the sun … . Every morning a family of wild turkeys announces its presence with a high-pitched, liquid clucking. They shit on the path and crane their long necks to look through the open door. No one is home. The roof sags towards the floor, and all the windows are broken. You remember this dwelling. It belongs to a dream world, on the edge of a forest of fallen stars.

When emptiness is possible,
Everything is possible;
Were emptiness impossible,
Nothing would be possible.

Words float to the surface of the paper, materializing as if written with invisible ink. They shimmer before me, and when I place the tip of my pen on one of their letters, I can feel it pulsate. These words are ready to reveal the story that I've always longed to write. All I have to do is to follow their lead, to go wherever they take me. With blind faith … . When I open my eyes, the words have faded from sight and I'm left facing a blank sheet of paper. This happens every time. I must be more unassuming. I must call forth the words again and ask them to live, breathe, and remain on the page.

Life is no different from nirvana,
Nirvana no different than life.
Life's horizons are nirvana's:
The two are exactly the same.

In the sand, the tracks of a possum head back to the twisted outlines of several macrocarpas. The possum would have come down to the beach at night to forage among the heaps of seaweed. Around the bay, on the crest of a hill overlooking the harbour, the sunlight warms three beer bottles that have been placed in front of a gravestone. By another grave, a plastic windmill leans to one side. The only sound is a dull clacking—an old woman, down below, pulls a dinghy on wheels across the mudflats … . Two hours later, in a back garden, a small boy climbs to the top of a ladder. 'Am I closer to the clouds?' he asks. 'Yes,' replies his father, 'You're closer to the clouds.'

This shifting anguish
Has no nature of its own;
If it did, how could it have a cause?
Deny emptiness and you deny
The origins of suffering.

Sitting in a parked car, with rain streaming down the windscreen, I watch the vacant lot, and the brick warehouse beyond, soften and dissolve. Painful fragments of a life, given a little space, work themselves free, rotate, and form another pattern. The rain stops falling. Wisps of steam rise from an abandoned umbrella … . A man parks his car on the outskirts of a deserted city. As the notes of a saxophone fade away, he puts a gun to his head. Or so it seems. Cut to the same man holding a cell phone. Perhaps he is speaking to someone he loves. Perhaps he is trying to reconfigure his pain. The soundtrack is silent. The camera pans across the vacant lot, and the film comes to an end.

Clinging is to insist on being someone –
Not to cling is to be free to be no one.

Among the first things ever photographed were: leaves of a plant, lace work, pieces of china, hydrangea flowers, trees and reflections, haystacks, brooms and spades … . The one who picked up a needle or swept a courtyard is nowhere to be found. But his daily actions, even her most fleeting gestures, continue to vibrate in the world. I can feel this as I stand before the departure gate and wave goodbye. I am disappearing. I am waving as I disappear. There is only the waving. Just a hand moving through space.

WRITING WITH ISSA

ripe persimmon,
overnight
the rat got it

The beginning of winter is warm on Great Barrier Island, and as well as a rat I have fleas and mosquitoes to keep me company in this remote cabin, which is to be my home for the next six weeks. While meditating upstairs one evening, a tiny spider suspends itself from the hood of my jacket and dangles in front of my eyes. I think of Issa, the most beloved of the Japanese haiku poets, who felt a great affinity for small things, especially insects. Nothing was too insignificant to be overlooked, and he wrote hundreds of verses on flies, mosquitoes, ants, spiders, crickets, silverfish, snails, lice, and fleas.

Issa was born Kobayashi Yataro in 1763, in the mountain village of Kashiwara in central Japan. Shortly after his second birthday, his mother died and he was raised by his grandmother. When Yataro turned eight, his father decided to remarry. His step-mother, who eventually gave birth to a son of her own, despised Yataro, and his childhood from then on became a torment. After six years of conflict within the family, the father sent his fourteen-year-old son to Edo to work as an apprentice for a literary man. In 1792, at the age of twenty-nine, Yataro vowed to follow the Way of Poetry, and changed his name to Issa, which means 'a cup of tea'.

Steam from my bowl of noodles surrounds the candle flame. Outside the night wind blows the screech of a morepork from tree to tree. I find myself writing with Issa, taking up a small selection of his haiku – verses that have stayed with me over the years – and adding a brief commentary to each one. In this way I grow closer to

Issa, and to his understanding of both the interconnectedness and the impermanence of all things.

*

in this world of dew
we walk on the roof of Hell
gazing at the flowers

Although Issa was born and died in the mountain country of Shinano, he spent the middle part of his life in Edo, the old name for Tokyo. At the beginning of the 19th Century, Edo was a bustling and overcrowded city, its wooden shops and houses tightly packed together. Fires regularly broke out, especially in the poorer quarters, and in 1806 Issa was forced to move several times when flames spread through the district in which he had settled. With rivers coloured red and smoke blackening the sky, it must have appeared to Issa that Hell itself had briefly come to earth.

Bearing this in mind, I can't help but think of that other fire which struck Japan in the middle of the 20th Century. No description by a writer removed in space and time can truly convey the effects of a nuclear holocaust. For accuracy and compassion it is better to read the first-hand accounts of the *hibakusha*, the survivors of the atomic bomb, in books like *Hiroshima Diary* and *We of Nagasaki*.

While visiting a friend on Great Barrier Island, I talked with her houseguest. He had just had two beers for breakfast, and with shaking hands he rolled himself a cigarette … . In our own life there are many small, barely noticeable fires which burn underground, untended and painful to endure.

Years ago I passed a man in the street. For a second our eyes met. His face was unshaven and the jacket he wore was faded and frayed. I caught no anguish in his expression; he just seemed distracted. But the way he held his head, to one side and bowed down, made me think that he had suffered a series of blows. At that moment another realm of existence was both revealed and eclipsed, as when a book is suddenly closed and you glimpse only a few words in the text; or when a piece of fabric is withdrawn under a door and you hear the rustling of a dress as it descends a flight of stairs … . I watched the small flames flicker around his form, around the people walking by, around the cars parked in the background, and the parking-meters, and the edges of the office buildings. Then he was gone. The red dissolved into grey, a uniform grey, and it began to rain.

*

children imitating cormorants
are even more wonderful
than cormorants

The rain transforms itself into a river; Japanese characters are transformed into English words; children translate themselves into cormorants. Everything is changing shape, becoming something else. And yet there is an underlying unity, a force or current that moves through all things. In rare moments slight but miraculous fluctuations can take us by surprise. And when our preconceived ideas fall away, our ordinary, predictable world is transformed.

In 1981 I was studying theatre at the Scuola Nuova Scena in Bologna. The curriculum included classes in acrobatics, clowning, and mime. Every few months we also attended a *serata*, an evening performance given by the school's second-year students. During one *serata*, a young Italian woman suddenly stood on her toes, rocked backwards, flung back her head, and released a series of high-pitched cries. She was not just imitating a dolphin; in one joyous burst of energy she had *become* a dolphin - tail slapping the water, body propelled fin-first through the air. This transformation only lasted a few seconds, but it was one of the most stunning things that I have ever seen.

A few months later, the same group of second-year students presented a one-act play. This time the young woman walked on stage as a prostitute. She was heavily made-up and wore a low-cut dress with a feather boa wrapped around her neck. I found her scene painful to watch; the essential was missing and only theatrical clichés remained. Sitting down on a chair, she had to listen to a male character, standing behind her, deliver a long and elaborate monologue. For the audience it was obvious that she felt uncomfortable in her role. But even though her vibrancy had been suppressed, the dolphin was still there, invisible beneath the surface. Given the right circumstances, the right causes and conditions, it would manifest itself again – unexpectedly and in another guise – to break through the waves.

*

insects on a bough
floating downriver
still singing

Issa's life could be described as a series of disasters. Having survived one set of rapids, with the sluggish current once more gaining speed, he is soon swept towards another outcrop of rocks.

In 1801 his father succumbed to typhoid fever and Issa returned home to nurse him. After the funeral, his step-mother and step-brother contested his father's will and Issa was deprived of his inheritance, the family property, for thirteen years. During that period he travelled back and forth from Edo to Kashiwara while engaged in litigation. He makes no direct reference to these conflicts in his writing, but his painful experience of the uncertainties of life would have sharpened his appreciation of the present moment. No doubt Issa identified with those small insects, singing singing singing as they were carried downstream.

A river runs past the cabin on Great Barrier Island. When the weather is fine, I write in the back garden. Clouds often gather overhead, raindrops patter down on my paper, words blur, and I'm forced to go indoors. M, the owner of the property, is on holiday in Australia. And although the cabin has been built at the bottom of a valley and receives little sunlight in winter, the sombreness inside is not due to the shadows alone; there is a sadness contained within its walls.

Today, while taking a tea-break, I pull out a copy of *The Barrier Bulletin*, the island's bi-monthly newspaper, from a pile of magazines. This issue is ten years old, and my eyes fall upon an article about a young resident who died in a car crash on the mainland. He turns out to be M's son. Accompanying the text is a photograph of friends spray-painting messages on his coffin. As I study the photograph, I feel the sadness of the cabin coming into focus. This young man, who was aged nineteen at the time, lived here and listened to the sound of the river, just as I'm listening to it now.

In the afternoon I hike downstream. At one crossing, a fantail flickers overhead and gives me an enthusiastic welcome. She's been picking midges out of the air. Now she chirps and trills and flits about. Full of life, just as the midges—white specks in the sunlight—are also full of life. They'll be safe for a few minutes, until the fantail loses interest in me.

*

simply trust,
do not the petals flutter down
just like that

In a self-portrait, Issa depicts himself as an odd, cold-looking figure, with his shoulders hunched up and his back turned away. But this is just an outward view; despite all that he had undergone, he retained a tender heart. In 1818, at the age of fifty-one, he married a young woman named Kiku. She gave birth to a son, who survived only a month. A second son was born and died the following year. Then their daughter, Sato, died of smallpox at the age of two. A third son was born in 1823, and both he and Kiku passed away a few months later. How does one live in the world after suffering such a series of losses? I don't know. But the same hand that smoothed hair from a child's brow and tucked in a blanket, also picked up a brush and wrote, 'simply trust ...'

A pink blossom from a puriri tree falls on the stone table beside my pen. It's strange to think that so large a tree sheds these small pale flowers. Winter is moving through the hills and down the valley. I shiver in the morning while cooking my porridge. But I have everything I need to continue with my work. Last evening I wrote a letter to the rat, asking him not to leave his turds on the kitchen bench. In return I said that I would put a little food for him outside each night. I then placed the letter—a single page with extra-large print—by the gas burner, where I knew he would find it on his nocturnal rounds. And in the morning all the kitchen surfaces were clean.

When I return to Auckland in a few weeks, things will not be so simple. But the city has its own continuity: buses still stop for passengers at bus stops; mail keeps on being delivered; food appears on the shelves of supermarkets. In spring, fireworks will briefly light up the night sky; by summer the smell of mildew will have begun to rise from the piles of old books in the secondhand bookshop at the end of the arcade; and on the balcony of a restored villa, an Alsatian dog will poke his head between the balustrades, as he did the year before, and bark frenetically as I walk past. This is sufficient; I will take the barking to be a confirmation. And afterwards, to see a sparrow or a fallen leaf will also be enough to keep me on the right track.

*

this world of dew
is a world of dew
and yet … and yet

Issa wrote this haiku on the death of Sato, his young daughter. The first two lines express the fundamental truth of Buddhism that everything in our life is impermanent, evanescent: animals, children, old people, husbands, wives, fathers, mothers … all arise and depart, disappearing into a great void. Nothing can bring them back. To know this is also to acknowledge the attachments we have formed while being alive, especially to those we love. This is why Issa hesitates; and his hesitation reminds us that we're human, that we're intimately connected to everything and everyone around us.

The outhouse is an A-framed structure, covered with chicken wire and open to the elements. For most of this week it has rained heavily during the night, and each morning, when I go to relieve myself, I find that a small spider has rebuilt her web in a new location. Today I watch her in action: as she revolves and spins her thread, she attaches it from the outside inward, each angular circuit taking less time to complete. And when the last strand is in place, she rests at the centre. The sun begins to rise over the eastern hills, and the web vibrates like a skeletal fingerprint.

So much work—a lifetime of work and effort and struggle .... In 1986 my mother suddenly died. Our last hours were spent together as she lay unconscious in her hospital bed, having undergone exploratory surgery. Night had fallen outside, and the fluorescent lights hummed faintly in her room. We spoke to her, but she couldn't respond, remaining deep within herself. A blood clot had formed on her right lung, and in the early morning her breathing became less and less. Amid the inner turmoil, amid the suddenness of everything, amid the waves of pain and love, Issa's verse came to mind. I took her hand, which was pale and swollen from a recent injection. And there, on the back of her hand, was a droplet of moisture, shining in the light.

*

this line of ants
continues continues
from the billowing clouds

Issa probably watched these ants on a summer's day while sitting in his back garden. Out of curiosity, he may have got up and opened the gate to see where they were coming from. Following their thin line, his eyes would glide up the slope of a hill, or over a rice paddy, to the clouds beyond. One commentator on this haiku, R.H. Blyth, observes that the linking of ants and clouds 'arises from Issa's childlike nature . . . the fairytale instinct in him.' A more rational voice might chip in with the fact that we know, from the reports of balloonists, how air currents can sweep ants, spiders, and mites into the upper atmosphere, along with pollen, seeds, and spores. But Issa's ants have not been randomly plucked into the air; they march forward with purpose from the white mass of the clouds themselves.

When it gets too cold to work in the shade of the back garden, I walk up the hillside and into the sunlight, establishing a writing-place for myself on the front deck of a new house that M has begun to construct. In the afternoon, from the top of the hill which dominates this valley, a giant, primitive face stares down at me. Shadows, cast by dense stands of trees, form his almond-shaped eyes, flared nostrils, and open mouth.

In the warm sunlight, a rippling plays along the deck's skirting boards; waves of black ants are moving back and forth. At the same time, more ants—hundreds of them—are streaming up and down the wooden walls, briefly touching antennae to exchange scent-information. There is something molecular about their activity; each one adheres to its own circuit while engaged in a series of contacts. The closer I look, the more the ants undermine the static appearance of the timber, suggesting that all solid forms are basically particles in motion.

Over the scowling hill, clouds are slowly changing shape. Elongated by the wind, they become streamlined, drawing their ragged fins and udders and forelegs back into their folds, smoothing out their bumps and wrinkles to assume a simpler form. I think of ant eggs for a moment, and then discard that thought. No, the clouds are just changing into clouds, drifting through a picture book of blue sky.

*

a butterfly in flight
and I below –
a creature of dust

After the death of his first wife, Issa remarried a year later, in 1824. His bride was from a samurai family and their marriage lasted only a few months. In 1827, at the age of sixty-four, Issa married Yao, a local mid-wife. The following year, his family home, which he had finally secured, caught fire and burned to the ground. In November of the same year, Issa died without warning, like a flash of autumn lightning or a bubble disappearing into a stream. His death deprived him of being present at the birth of his only surviving child, a daughter named Yata.

In the haiku above, Issa feels his own mortality as he contrasts his earth-bound existence to the freedom of a butterfly. The lightness of the verse—and lightness is intrinsic to Issa's writing—is tempered by a note of sadness, and even of envy. But being a follower of the Buddha, Issa would know that there is fundamentally no separation between himself and the butterfly. For their part, insects also age. In this fleeting world, the wings of a butterfly can be seen as membranes of coloured dust (there are moths so delicate that they dissolve at the touch of a finger). We are all masses of particles; when we die, either consumed by fire or buried in the ground, these particles intermingle with others, and the energy released by our atoms continues on.

At the beginning of the year, driving around the North Island, I visited a number of *pa* sites, Maori fortifications which played a central role in the New Zealand Wars. While exploring the earthworks of Te Kooti's redoubt in the Tongariro National Park, a giant dragonfly flashed past. Stretching out my arm, the dragonfly returned to settle on the back of my hand. It remained there for several minutes as I walked above the trenches, allowing me to admire its long, ebony- and ivory-striped body and its large, multifaceted eyes. I noticed that the top of its thorax, just behind its swivelling head, was going bald, and that its wing-joints were worn down from constant use. Its transparent wings also revealed a number of tears, and in all probability this impressive insect was nearing the end of its life.

Around us, nothing remained of the fierce fighting that took place between the government forces and their Maori allies on one side, and Te Kooti's warriors on the other. The geometry of the redoubt had become blurred by long grass. And the only sound to be heard, on that summer's day, was the humming of bees in the white-flowering manuka.

*

spring rain:
a rat is lapping
the Sumida River

I caught a glimpse of my rat this evening as he disappeared into the woodpile by the kitchen door. He's a native rat, a *kiore,* with a shortish tail and brown fur. Our agreement to keep the kitchen clean only lasted three days; now he's back to depositing a few turds on the bench at night. For my part, I forgot to leave him some food scraps, and sometime after midnight he dragged away a bar of Sunlight soap. But it is mid-winter, and I reflect, while switching off the gas burner and filling my hot-water bottle, that all creatures do what they can to stay alive.

Two hundred years ago, Issa observed another rat, who had made his way to the edge of the Sumida River. Under the falling rain, which would have provided some shelter from predators above, the rat bent down to drink, his delicate ears pricked up to detect any sound beyond the surging of the current and the pattering of raindrops. And just as the river entered the rat, the rat entered the river, becoming a part of its history, a part of its life. At that moment, with its pink hands (so much like miniature versions of our own) resting on a pebble or a matting of reeds, the rat held the river in place, stitching it to a particular day in spring as it lapped up the cool, transparent waters with the smallest of tongues.

My own river, which is really more of a stream, continues to flow past the cabin. Seated on my meditation cushion, I listen to how its many voices engage themselves in one long and harmonious conversation. No detail is omitted, no leaf or rock or insect. And when I sit with Issa, the sound of the water, in different tones and textures, repeats the same message over and over again …

TIME AND LIGHT

(During one summer in Rochester, I was on wake-up duty at the Zen Center. Just before dawn, I would take the hand-bell out of its cupboard in the kitchen and begin my rounds, pausing briefly on the walkway to observe the sunrise.)

The pebbles slowly become a soft gray, emerging out of their pools of shadows. Each one—a few minutes ago just part of an anonymous border beneath the eaves of the house—is now rounded and distinct. The early morning light also reveals the cracks in the brick path and the slats of the wooden benches, which have been placed seemingly at random around the garden. The trunks and branches of the small trees appear black against the grass, and their leaves, separating themselves from the buildings in the background, begin to rustle in the breeze. High up on the underside of a fire-escape, the steel rungs glow pink as if the metal were being heated by an invisible flame.

I stand on the covered walkway for a moment, glancing down at my watch then back to the garden and the subtly changing intensities of light. Squirrels have yet to come out, and the raccoons, which I have only heard about but never seen, remain hidden or are foraging elsewhere. As 5:12 slips into 5:13, I open the door that leads to the dormitories. Breathing in, I begin to ring the hand-bell—not too hard, not too soft. Nevertheless, the sound of bright metal erases the silence, shatters it, before being covered by silence again.

In the kitchen the slices of cantaloupe have been placed upright around the inside of a large wooden bowl and form what appears to be a conference of crescent moons, their opaque flesh a pale orange in the sunlight, which is also shining through the honey in the honey dispensers and spreading itself across the varnished surface of the table. The grains in the wood stand out like slivers of metal, and the white china bowls, arranged in a line, become even whiter as the sound of early morning traffic increases in the background.

But this scene is two hours away. I return time to its correct sequence, ringing the bell throughout the main house at 5:15. A strip of light lies under one door like a solid bar. Another threshold is dark, the room closed, its occupant wrenched out of sleep the moment I walk past. Then, in an empty room at the end of the passageway, the luminous glow of a digital clock is visible in the darkness. As the number six disappears into the number seven on the right-hand side of the clock-face, I finish my rounds. From a nearby bathroom there's the lingering smell of shampoo, and the sound of teeth being brushed.

Downstairs in the zendo, the two small windows at the far end glow with a cool blue light. Spaced between the round cushions, which sit quietly on their brown mats, loom larger forms: attenuated tree-stumps or outcrops of rock, each one immersed in its own silence. At a certain point, the lights overhead are turned up so that the walls emit a subdued orange, a warmth in which the upright shapes are revealed to be what they have always been: people seated in meditation. Outside a dog barks, on and off. The front door of a house slams shut, followed a few seconds later by the door of a car. In a bush below the window, sparrows chirp in unison, as though stirred up by the wind. And the night, now almost over, retreats to the thin black line of material that marks the edge of the tatami matting.

Another hand rings another bell. Three clear notes. One long round of meditation then unfolds, with chanting at the end, after which breakfast is eaten and the workday begins.

To relax, in the late afternoon, I sit outside a café and slowly consume a lemon ice. A brief shower of rain has left the sidewalk dark and damp. But overhead the sky is without a cloud. Time has become diffuse; the seconds and minutes drift apart. And if anyone were to ask me what this practice is—this practice of Zen—I would have to say:

It's simply the pleasure
of watching patches of sunlight and shadows
glide over the coat of an old man
as he walks beneath the linden trees.

THE BODHISATTVIC GARDEN

(After the zendo, the Zen Center's back garden is an ideal place for contemplation. It remains a still point in the middle of an inner-city neighbourhood, and when I need to begin a letter, or to make some notes on the changing seasons, I find myself drawn to its domain.)

Today, having nothing to write down, I leave my notebook open on one of the tables. As the pages flutter in a light breeze, the white paper with its thin blue lines absorbs the chattering of nearby sparrows, the scuttling of a squirrel as it spirals down a tree trunk, the flickering of someone walking briskly behind a fence. High up in the late afternoon sky, the vapour trail of a plane, reflecting the earth, becomes more elongated and curved as it stretches towards the horizon.

The following evening, the neighbour's calico cat presses her nose against the screen door and stares across the kitchen foyer into the twilight of the zendo. Like a person admiring a painting by Vermeer, she studies the receding aisle of shadowy figures who are sitting in perfect stillness on their brown cushions. Then a bell is struck to end the round of meditation, and she disappears down the back steps, her own bell tinkling faintly as she runs across the lawn.

*

The leaves are whispering to each other in a light and steady rain. Summer is now well-established, and the covering of myrtle under the locust tree is a deep shade of green. Beyond the myrtle, a dogwood is in full bloom, its white, four-leafed flowers resembling clusters of child-like stars. Overhead, hidden by the foliage, a crow caws twice and then falls silent. The dry pebbles under the eaves of the covered walkway seem whiter than usual. And the rain continues, discreetly, accompanied by the rustling of sparrows.

The next day the rain is forgotten (winter itself being only a memory), and the whole garden radiates a steady and reassuring heat. For work, three people are stuffing cushions on the back deck. At one point a large clump of kapok is carried away by a gust of wind, only to be caught in the branches of a nearby fir tree. It stays there for a while before being dislodged by another gust of wind, which sends it rolling across the lawn. Sparrows, attentive to any change in the garden, soon surround the clump, plucking wisps from its white mass. A thick covering of clouds remains overhead. In the background, someone is hammering in nails; it's the time for repairing roofs as well as for making nests.

*

An early evening in mid-September. The seasons have begun to change, and I'm sitting on a bench in the back garden. The light is gently luminous. A warm breeze, descending through the branches of a maple tree, also rises up from the lawn. It's as though I've dipped my feet in the invisible waves of a departing summer, and I feel myself becoming lighter, even as the evening sky begins to shed its light.

A month later, after the first frost, crickets are still chirping beneath the earth. One afternoon, while sitting on the walkway, I study the progress of a solitary bee as it moves through the cold air, slowly and methodically exploring the lawn. From my vantage point, it's plain to see that all the flowers have gone, and that there's not a speck of white or yellow to be found among the blades of grass. Nevertheless, the bee continues its exploration. In doing so, it displays the same perseverance as a lone firefly who kept vigil in the garden one night in mid-summer. For half an hour, although no other light responded, I watched its green pulse flicker on and off as the firefly wove its way above the bushes and between the trees.

*

During the night, the sparrows' water dish outside our window froze over, and today it's capped by a dome of white. In the back garden, the upper part of each tree branch – now completely leafless – is covered by a line of snow, so that it seems as if a shift in focus has occurred, or that a white tree has been superimposed over every dark one. For their part, each of the benches has its own mound of snow. They resemble a collection of small tombs; soft structure into which you can insert your hand and touch – not a piece of bone – but the finest lining of crystals.

For the Rohatsu sesshin, at the beginning of December, I'm the receptionist. During the day I work in the office, opening mail and answering telephone calls. This afternoon, mid-way through the sesshin, the temperature plummets, and snowflakes the size of white butterflies come down. When I go outside, the snow suddenly stops, the sky lightens, and dense flocks of crows begin flying overhead. I follow the crows into Arnold Park, where they're already roosting in every tree. By this time, part of the sky in the distance is pure blue, while overhead it remains a pearly gray. You can see how green the grass is – luminous and aquatic – beneath the fresh covering of snow, and how the windows of the houses along one side of the street are being transformed into sheets of burning gold by the setting sun. But most intoxicating of all are the voices of the crows in the trees around me: cawing, barking, yelping, screeching, giving little trills and peeps and whistles, croaking like bullfrogs, chattering like kookaburras, going off like car alarms, gurgling like old drainpipes … and whispering darkly as if night has just fallen. Mixed in with this, you can also hear the *Heart Sutra* being chanted by fifty people from inside the zendo:

Form is only emptiness, emptiness only form.

As I stand by the gate, about to enter the silence of the back garden, a crow flies past with snow on its beak. 'The garden hears the cries of the world,' I will later write in my notebook. 'It provides a setting, a locus, where all things can rest and be resolved.'

HEADWORX

Series Editor: Mark Pirie

New Poetry

Nothing to Declare Harry Ricketts
Salamanca Vivienne Plumb
Sweet Banana Wax Peppers Jenny Powell-Chalmers
The Century Tony Beyer
Pingandy Harvey McQueen
Unmanned Stephen Oliver
Earth Colours L E Scott
Talking Pictures Riemke Ensing
Hats Jenny Powell-Chalmers
Rhyme Before Reason Scott Kendrick
abstract internal furniture Helen Rickerby
Night of Warehouses Stephen Oliver
Our Bay of Ensigns Bernard Gadd
The Snow Poems/your self of lost ground Jeanne Bernhardt
Storyteller Simon Williamson
Boat People Tim Jones
Chantal's Book Jack Ross
The Ballad of Fifty-one Bill Sewell
Toku Tinihanga (Self Deception) Michael O'Leary
Maketu Terry Locke
How to Occupy Our Selves David Howard & Fiona Pardington
The Year Nothing Paul Hardacre
Summer on the Côte d'Azur Alistair Paterson
Recessional Harvey McQueen
Over the Waters Moshé Liba
Natural Anthem Leonard Lambert
Four French Horns Jenny Powell-Chalmers
Here and There Basim Furat
Nefarious Vivienne Plumb
Make Love and War Michael O'Leary
Your Secret Life Harry Ricketts
Daymoon Robin Fry
Suchness Richard von Sturmer*